# CALLED

# TO

# INTERCEDE

## Volume 8

By
## Dr. Monique Rodgers & An Elite Army of
## Intercessors and Prayer Warriors

Foreword by
Dr. Tamike Brown

United States of America

Published by Shooting Stars Publishing House 2022
Copyright © 2022 Dr. Monique Rodgers

ISBN:9788447067779

# DEDICATION

This book is dedicated to children. You are in our forever prayers.

# CONTENTS

# FOREWORD

**Dr. Tamike Brown**

**The Breath & Wind Of The Intercessor**

Called To Intercede "Praying for Children" is written by a collaborative team of Intercessors who has been called to the frontline to intercede in prayer. As our world is changing daily at a rapid pace the time of urgency calls for praying to include praying for the children all around the world. Intercessors values and understands the importance to pray for children as they face these day-to-day changes to cope with life mechanisms. In this new world century children are experiencing things they never thought they would ever have to experience before in their life; whereas some has committed suicide or taken on suicidal thoughts from the mental issues that attack their minds.

The bible tells us children are a heritage unto the Lord; meaning God sees children as being a gift and incredibly special to Him that holds an untouchable place in His Heart. Therefore, it is very vital as a team of Intercessors to cover the children in prayer. Prayer can go where you and I cannot go. Prayer can do what you and I cannot do because prayer reaches the very throne room God who hears and answer all prayers including the ones we pray for the children.

After reading this book of prayers as parents or an Intercessor called to Intercede, I pray you will understand the importance of praying for children and for God to give you the strength to never give up on your children no matter how tough the battle may seem. Continue to stand strong in the Word of God praying and interceding for your children covering them by the blood of Jesus every day. Never give up praying for the children because you just might be the only Jesus they will ever see until they come into the saving knowledge of Jesus Christ for themselves. Represent Christ and always know that prayer changes things.

Many thanks to Dr. Monique Rodgers who God saw fit as the visionary to bring the Intercessors together from all around the world as team to intercede in prayer for the children. To God be the Glory!


Dr. Tamike Brown

Tamike Brown Ministries

Atlanta, Georgia

# ABOUT THE INTERCESSOR

## TRISH SMITH-WHITING

My name is Trish Whiting. I am married to Larry Whiting of 9 years. We have two children MarSadie (7) and JaMarius (19). I accepted Jesus as my Lord and Savior at the age of five. I currently reside in Muncie, IN. I was a member of Antioch Baptist Church since five but now I am a member of Deliverance Temple under the leadership and guidance of Pastor Andre Mitchell and 1st Lady Devon Mitchell.

# CHAPTER 1

# Mother's Prayer

## Trish Smith Whiting

Father God In the Name of Jesus. I first want to say thank you for being God all by oneself. Father God, I thank you for life, health, strength. God, I want to say thank you for the opportunity to cry out before you God. I Thank you for the privilege to bare, raise, adopt, and have children. I thank you God for the children that are not biologically mine but are growing up as soldiers for your ARMY

GOD. I thank you God for the mother that had to give up the child to CPS or had to have the child removed for the protection of your soldier (the child). Jesus, I want to just thank you for this prayer that will go before thousands and touch the hearts of millions. Father God, I ask that as you go into the homes of the children that are being raised Father God, I ask that you touch the mother, father, grandmother, grandfather, and guardian. God, I ask that you begin to minister to them, lead them, and guide them to come to you God. I know that it starts with you dear God and so that we as parents, guardians, grandparents would turn our hearts back to you so we can raise our children in the admiration of you Father God. Jesus, I ask that as you restore wisdom, knowledge and understanding back to the parents, caretakers, guardians, grandparents. God, I ask that the knowledge begins to flow to the children and began to regenerate a generation that is hungry after your righteousness. I ask that you lead and guide the children as a General leads an Army. I ask you to lead them like you did for Moses as he was leading the Israelites that were chased by Pharaoh's army out of Egypt and God you kept and protected them. I ask that you keep the children from dangers seen and unseen. God, I ask that you would be with the child or children that facing identity crisis and do not know where they stand. God, I ask that you show them who they are in you and that will keep that child from wondering in the wilderness of struggles, unhealthy relationships, wanting validation from invalidated world. God, I ask you to cover that single mother, father, that when they were given the seed to bare children, they are left raising them by them self. God, I ask you to be with them, provide for them, God, I ask you to show yourself strong where there is a weak spot. Father God, I ask that you give and fulfill every need financially, emotionally, and spiritually need. God, I ask that you touch the child that has been birth from an addiction. God, I ask that you heal the child's body that may be born into trauma from a drug addicted mother or father. Jesus, I ask that you show yourself unto the mother or father to stop the addiction for the life of the unborn child. Jesus, I know that you can do it.

According to Ephesians 3:20 New Living Translations says: "Now all glory to God, who is able, through your mighty power at work within us, to accomplish infinitely more than we might ask or think. God you can do exceedingly, abundantly above all that we could ask or think. Father God, I just ask you to cover the children or children whose parent has emotionally traumatized a child or children because of a generational curse. God, I stand in the gap and break the back of the curse. I cut your head off and I bury you in the spirit in the Name of Jesus. The spirit of molestation no longer is hidden in the homes of our child or children. God, I bind that spirit and send it back to the pit of hell from which it belongs. JESUS! JESUS! JESUS! We call out to you because through you I have the ability and strength I denounce the spirit that has laid dormant for days, years, centuries, decades. Repair God. Restore God. Set free God. God I just ask that you hear my prayers. God, I ask that you translate what my heart is speaking to pray for the children. I ask God that you be honored, and I ask God that you be glorified. I know God by your stripes we are healed. I declare your stripes over the child or children who have fallen into any of my heart desires whether spoken or unspoken. Jesus, I give you all the glory the honor and the praise. JESUS! God your worthy of all the glory, the honor, and the praise. I submit these requests before you as a petition that will continue to flow from the mouth and heart as a desire to who may read this. It is so In JESUS name Amen.

# ABOUT THE INTERCESSOR

## Minister Katina Allbrook-Logan

Minister Katina Allbrook-Logan is a blessed and anointed Woman of God. She is a wife, a mother, a grandmother, and an advocate for her community. She is a junior at Strayer University. She is a graduate of Mercy High School. She has served on many auxiliaries for several years as a Singer, Praise and Worship Leader, Sunday School Teacher, and Hospitality Leader. She became a Cancer Care Minister in Philadelphia in 2018, after overcoming Breast Cancer. She has completed Leadership Christian counseling. Later she became an ordained Minister in November 2020. She is an Ambassador for Kingdom Sniper Institute.

# Chapter 2

# Leading My Example in Prayer

## Minister Katina Allbrook-Logan

This Chapter is dedicated to: My children, my grandchildren, and all the children who have no one to intercede for them. From my heart to yours, this chapter is for you. I love you all with the love of the Lord.

I want to thank Dr. Monique Rodgers for this opportunity for listening and hearing my testimonies as being a child and prayed my way through life. She compelled me to get started where my heart has been for years. That is with the children.

I want to thank my husband Anthony Logan for having a heart of a child, so I will always remain humble on how to talk, treat, and honor him for being a child of God. I love you and thank you for sharing your child like heart with me and my family. I will forever be so grateful. Titus 2:4

These older women must train the younger women to love their husbands and their children. The bible tells us in Ephesians 6:1-4, Children, obey your parents in the Lord: for this is right. What if your earthly parents are not obeying God? What do you do?

Children yearn to seek the love and direction from others once they come out the womb. They yearn to be cuddled, swaddled, fed, clothed, held, and bathed by a loved one. Children sense the affections or rejections once they are held. As children get older, they tend to feed off others by watching others do what they do.

They mimic behaviors that are surrounded by them continuously. Some behaviors come from genetic genes, or DNA, some children can also display behaviors that are generational.

The Bible says in Ephesians 5:1-Be ye therefore followers of God, as dear children. Walk in love, as Christ also hath loved us, and hath given himself for us an offering and a sacrifice to God for a sweetsmelling savior.

Children walk in love so pure and innocent. They demonstrate the love of Christ Jesus early. Children are showing us the way to get to Jesus. However, because we are the adults, we tend to tell them when they are right and when they are wrong. If we as adults do not know the word of God or the Lord's prayer, how can we lead them to God?

Did you know the Lord will answer a child's cry or prayer quicker than ours? Children do not have nothing standing in their way to get to God when they are young. After a certain age, once you understand the meaning of giving yourself to the Lord, we must seek the kingdom and all his righteousness.

Let us start with…

## The Lord's Prayer: Matthew 6:9-13 Version (KJV)

Our Father which art in heaven, Hallowed be thy name. Thy kingdom come, thy will be done on earth, as it is in heaven. Give us this day our daily bread. And forgive us our debts, as we forgive our debtors. And lead us not into temptation but deliver us from evil:

For thine is the kingdom, and the power, and the glory, forever. Amen.

The bible says in John 3:16 For God so loved the world that he gave his one and only Son, that whoever believes in him shall not perish but have eternal life.

How many people would give their children away to the world as a living sacrifice? I believe many people already have given their children away to the world to lead the way for them. The world's way is not the way to God.

We have given our children so many things to entertain them and their minds away from their Salvation. Giving them the freedom of choice in using Cell phones, games, videos, lots of tv and computer time, and even sports and hobbies for some. We are quick to drop them off to family, friends, and even to college with the expectation of them to do the impossible and raise our children for us. The bible tells us that we must train our children in the way they are supposed to go, they will not depart from it.

## Let us pray… For Direction:

"Father in the name of Jesus, I come to you on behalf of our children and their mindsets. I pray that our children will find you early in life so they may have a better chance in surviving in these last and evil days. I pray that we as a people can lift our children up to you and you will hear from us as the intercessors and answer our prayers for the children. Lead us and guide us Lord, as we ask for direction to be deposited into our hearts and minds in the mighty name of Jesus. I ask you to cover our children daily and here our prayers Lord,

Amen."

God desires us to seek him first so we do not move and operate from our own self will for his children. If God has blessed you with

11

children, then he will guide you with many scriptures in the bible regarding children. Here is where you can begin to ask and seek direction for your children daily.

Follow parent's example: Genesis 26:7-11

Teaching them to follow God-Exodus 10:2, Deuteronomy 6:7, 31:10-

13, Psalms: 22:30-31, Psalms 78:5

How they are affected by the sins of their parents-Exodus 34:7

Parent-child relationships-Numbers 30:3-8, 1 Samuel 8:1-3

Preparing children to full fill God's call-1 Chronicles 22:7-10

A blessing from God-1 Chronicles 26:5, Psalms 127:3-5

Discipline of children-1 Kings 1:6 (2), Proverbs 13:24

Avoid complaining in front of children-2 Chronicles 10:14

Importance of obeying God at an early age 2 Kings 22:1-2

Pray for them-Job 1:5 (2)

Encouraging them to follow wisdom-Proverbs 4:3-4

Teaching them to make their choices-Proverbs 22:6

Teaching life lessons you have learned Joel 1:3

Hard for parents to let them go-Luke 2:48

Jesus welcomed them-Mark 9:36-37

Having faith like a child-Mark 10:14

Being childlike verses childish-Matthews 18:1-4

Our responsibility to instruct them in faith-Matthews 18:6, 2 Tim

3:15

They have the kind of attitude needed to approach God-Matthews

19:13-15

God's will for them verses parents will for them-Matthews 20:20(2)

Important to God-Acts 23:16-22

Purpose of parental discipline-Ephesians 6:4

Believers are God's children-1 John 3:1

These scriptures are a guide to help us to guide our hearts and minds to teach our children how to honor and receive God. I pray as you set your mind on Jesus as your Lord and Savior, allow the Holy Spirit to lead and guide you in spirit and in truth. I pray you will teach and share the love of Jesus to a child you may meet. I pray that you will share the love of Christ by leading by example. In Jesus name, Amen.

# ABOUT THE INTERCESSOR

## Kierra Fenn

Kierra Fenn is the Assistant Director of Outreach International Foundation Ministry, Kierra's Children Academy Radio & TV Show, and Co-Owner of TKKJ Video & Audio Production Company, based out of Atlanta Georgia. She loves God with everything within her and believes in the Power of God's Holy Word and there is nothing too hard for God.

She is the daughter of Dr. Tamike Brown and Father Mr.

Bobby Fenn. She was born in Cordele Georgia and raised in Atlanta GA where she currently resides. She graduated from Starr's Mill High School and Continued her education in Early Childhood Development receiving her degree at Central Georgia Technical College in Macon Georgia.

She has labored in the ministry field for many years alongside with her mother Dr. Evangelist Tamike Brown, and her two brothers

Kerwin Fenn, and Joshua Brown. She has a love for all people, enjoys winning souls to the Kingdom of God, and an extended passion for younger children in seeing them being a part of God's Kingdom. She also enjoys praising and worshiping God and is an obedient, respectful, loving, and kind person anyone could ever meet. She has a very humble Spirit with a servant heart and is willing to serve in whatever capacity needed in accomplishing the Will of God. In addition, she enjoys praying and interceding for others in going beyond the call of duty. She is a citizen of the Kingdom of God and grew up as part of the body of World Changers Ministries in Atlanta Georgia for many years. Currently she is a part of the local church body Temple of Prayer Family Worship Cathedral in Fairburn, GA under the leadership of Bishop Aaron B. Lackey Sr., and First Lady Lakita Lackey. Outside of God her biggest inspirational leader is her Mother Dr. Evangelist Tamike Brown. She says her mother has taught her so many things and cared for her in ways no one can even imagine. One day she believes the Father will allow her to tell her testimony story as to how God brought her through that will be an aide in winning more souls to the Kingdom of God. Finally, one of her dreams is to manage and operate a large daycare academy center for young children of parents who is in the mission field doing the Lord's Will as an extension of Outreach International Foundation Ministry. To God be the glory!

Chapter 3

# Children Are a Gift from God

**Kierra Fenn**

Children are a gift from God. It is important to raise children in the atmosphere of the Lord so they can grow and be developed in the word of God. When children become older in age they will know how to stand on the word of God when they are going through different things in their lives knowing that the word of God will give them hope. Children needs to know they are special in the eyesight of the Lord and that they are somebody and they can cry out to the Father and go to the Father about anything because God said forbid not the little children to come to Him. Children are a priority in the eyesight of God.

When God gives you a child or children know that the child is a gift from God. And when a gift is given, the gift is giving to you willingly. You did not have to pay for it. Therefore, when God gives parents children as a gift, He expects the parents to take care of the gift by nourishing the gift, cherishing the gift, loving the gift, teaching the children about the Giver of the gifts who is God Himself as God will provide everything the parents needs to raise that child. God expects parents to impart the word of God into the children life so they will know to respect and honor God as their Heavenly Father. They will know He is someone they can always call on even if their mother or father forsakes them.

When children are taught, they are a gift from God they will feel safe and protected in times of trouble. They will feel comfort when they are hurting or in pain knowing God is right there by their sides to bring them through every situation. They will hear the father voice saying I am with you. I am holding you. I will be a fence all around you. Nothing will harm you. And most important they will hear God say I love you.

It is important to teach children how to pray and worship the Lord not only during trying times or when they are going through, but they need to pray and worship God all the time. Giving him all the praise, the glory, and the honor. Children can learn these things when they see the parents honoring and worshipping God by reading the word of God and spending quality time in the presence of God. Children learn things quickly at an early age which is the best time to train a child. You cannot go wrong with training and teaching the children the word of God while they are small.

Here is an example of a prayer a child can pray concerning their school education.

Thank you, Heavenly Father, that you strengthen me in school to learn and understand the schoolwork my teacher asks me to do. Help me Father to study and learn so I can be an "A" plus honor roll student. God, I want to make good grades in school in all my class subjects, but I am having a tough time with understanding math and history, and I need you to help me, Lord. I pray Lord that I am encouraged and focused so I can make better grades in school. And Father please help my teacher to be nice and patient with me while I am trying to understand the work, she gives me. She has been very mean to me alot of times and it makes me incredibly sad. So, Father

I pray that you will protect and watch over my teacher, encourage her, love her, and heal her from whatever she is going through so she can be a better teacher to me and the other students in class in Jesus name amen.

As the Father has stated children are a gift from Him and they need to be taught to always have faith in God and trust God no matter what the situation is and whatever trials they may be going through. Be willing to always trust God. I pray the children will seek first the Kingdom of God and His righteousness and then God will add all things unto the children and give them the desires of their heart that will bring God Glory. I pray the children will be strong in the Lord and be a bold witness for Christ no matter where they go. Children can also be a witness for Christ in help winning other children to the Lord. They can encourage and tell their friends or classmates about who God is and how God saved and cares for them. How He helped he or she in school and how they can pray and go to God about anything, and He will be right there to help them. They can help others know and understand that He is the light of the world, and they are a gift from God even in a troubled world and the light of God will still shine bright and He will always be there to love and care for them.

I want to encourage parents to never turn your back on your children. Do not give up on your children even when you do not understand what they are going through. Be willing to cherish the gifts of your children as they are a gift from God. Show them always love because you are displaying the love of God when you love your children. Always pray for your children because there is a lot of peer pressure children go through in wanting to be accepted by other children. And encourage your children by letting them know that they are somebody and they are incredibly special to God and to you.

Children are a gift from God.

Kierra's Children Academy

https://outreachintfound.com/kierras-children-academy-radio-tv-show/ https://outreachintfound.com/

# ABOUT THE INTERCESSOR

## Minister Shaquatta Edgar

God called Minister Shaquatta Edgar to be a Chosen

Defender for the people. She is anointed to lead and intercede. She is a mother and has her own podcast in which she prays and speaks with boldness, confidence, and her God given authority. She is a flame thrower in the Holy Ghost.

Shaquatta is birthing all that God has placed on the inside of her. She is walking in her now and reaching out and snatching souls from the grips of hell with the love of God. She started Greater Love Ministries in her home and has led many nightly devotionals and prayer.

Her tribulations have prepared her to be the minister she needs to be to reach the world. She keeps fighting no matter what she has been through because she is an overcomer. Shaquatta is an author and a writer for Gifted Magazine. This global influencer is soaring higher in God to fulfill the works of the Kingdom. Keep up with this Chosen Defender because God is doing a magnificent work in her.

Chapter 4

# Prayers for the Unborn

## Minister Shaquatta Edgar

Who else could know any of us better than we know ourselves? It is the Lord God Almighty! Not only does He know us best, but He knew us first. It is Her that gave us life. We were more than just a fetus in the womb. We were a creation of the Highest God. My divine assignment is to be a voice that will cry out for souls that are lost and help lead them to Christ. Today, more has been added to that assignment. Prayers for the unborn that are already in the womb of many women waiting to give birth must be made. Also, prayers for those that have yet to be conceived from this generation to the next. Together, we must stand in the holy gap for them and reach the heart of God with our prayers.

We are reminded in the book of Jeremiah 1:5 that before we were formed in the womb of our mothers God knew us. To the unborn I say to you today, that you matter. You have significance and you shall make a significant difference in life. You have been set apart by your creator and appointed to do magnificent things in the earth. God took His time creating you and shaped you and molded you with both unique physical and mental qualities. When God created you, He breathed His very breath inside of you. Every thought that God has towards you are of peace. So do not worry He got you. No evil will come near you, only God's goodness and mercy will be upon you. It shall follow you all the days of your life and your latter days shall be greater than you are beginning.

No fear will be able to stop you from going forth. Whatever God gives you to speak will be spoken and proclaimed. Your mouth has been touched by the Lord's hands. Power has been placed inside of you that no man can take away. Before your mother carried you or will carry you, it is God that carried you first. So, you were never alone. God was with you, and with you He will always be. For you were created in His very likeness and image. You will not be distracted by the physical attributes or resemblance you have from your mother and father. You shall know that you belonged to God first and shall walk in His ways to trample over all that life throws your way. You are God's magnificent masterpiece. You shall have dominion over all that is in the earth and overcome any obstacle that is sent your way.

Sickness will not be able to overtake you in the womb because you have a savior that was beaten with many stripes and bore every infirmity in His body just for you. Generational sickness and poverty will not be your portion, but good health and wealth belongs to you. Generational trauma will not affect you. Every assignment of the enemy concerning you and your blood line pertaining to bullying, rape, molestation, physical abuse, mental abuse, and verbal abuse is cancelled. You will not be the receiver or the giver of such things.

I speak to the fruitful womb do not abort what you are carrying. For what you are carrying is precious cargo sent by God.

What you are carrying shall be great. What you are carrying is holy.

He or she can neither be bought or sold by man for they were already purchased with the blood of Christ. Your baby shall leap in your womb for joy. When you unload this cargo, you shall experience joy and gladness, and many will rejoice with you. I speak nothing but blessings and favor to you that carry such a powerful one in your womb.

What manner of child shall this be that you carry? The child that you carry will seek God's presence and forever glorify His name. Your child will be sober minded, disciplined, and filled with the Holy Ghost. Even at an early age they will also lead other children to the Lord and cause the unbelieving to understand and walk upright. They will be strong in Spirit and will not have an identity crisis for they will know exactly who they are and whose they are. All those that are in darkness your son, your daughter is the one that will lead them to light.

When your son or daughter is faced with adversity they will not run away. They will stand and call unto the Lord. They will remember what Moses spoke unto Joshua, to be strong and very courageous. They will remember not to turn away from the word of God, but they will meditate on the word day and night and do what is written therein so their way will be prosperous, and they will have good success. They will not be afraid because they will know God is with them wherever they go. (Joshua 1:7-9)

As a parent myself I have learned to speak positive words over my child. Even when the behavior is not so good, I must remember that she is still learning. I am the teacher at home that never packs away the lesson plan. Every day as a mother has not been great. Sometimes as a parent we blame ourselves for things that are beyond our control. This is where my knees touch the floor the most. There were days when I felt like what I prayed for was a waste of time, but every prayer shall be fulfilled. Why I ask do I have to keep going to this school to meet the principal. I already know the answer. Oh, do I know. It is more spiritual than natural. When the enemy see that he cannot have you he will go after your children.

Therefore, it is important to pray for and with our children. Never stop interceding for your child.

Our children should see and hear us praying. If you are a mother or a father, I encourage you to do this and never stop. They are watching us now more than ever. You know you are being an example to them when they see lightening, hear thundering, and start to pray. I laughed when I heard my nine-year-old daughter praying for the storm to pass, but she was not laughing when she was praying. She was so serious, so serious that she prayed for the storm to pass twice. We did not get blown away by the storm and our home is still intact. We both got to experience the fruit of that prayer. I smile with joy because she is growing up so amazingly fast before my eyes and learning so much. It was yesterday that she was in my womb, and I was singing to her gospel melodies. I will never forget those beautiful eyes wide open shining back at me, when she was supposed to be crying but instead, she was smiling. She asks me about a lot that I may not remember but that day I remember. I still have so much I want to teach her about our Lord. Some days I minister to her and some days she minsters to me. She loves to talk so there is no doubt in my mind that she will be used even the more as a mouthpiece for God. Queen, as she is already called shall lead many from darkness to light and so shall your king or queen.

# ABOUT THE INTERCESSOR

**Kayla Gordon**

J.B Kayla is an author, entrepreneur, and youth leader. God has chosen her to break generational curses. She was born and raised on the westside of Chicago, Illinois. She is a thirteen-year-old young lady who has a passion to write and inspire through life lessons. Kayla is the youngest of her mom's five children. Although young, she is incredibly wise and has alot to offer to those who listen. Kayla has witnessed many homeless individuals and has grown a passion to help them however she can. One of Kayla's life goals is to own a boutique and salon where she specializes in custom makeovers for homeless and less fortunate individuals. She wants them to know no matter what they are special, not alone, and God loves them despite their situation. Kayla enjoys public speaking and opportunities to encourage others. She enjoys spending time with family and close friends and hopes that her children's book will encourage children her age not to bully and if they are a victim of being bullied, Speak Up!

# Chapter 5

# Prayer Means Everything to Me

## Kayla Gordon

Prayer is a good thing. It is especially important to me because it helps people. It can help you in dangerous situations. Prayer can help also help others who get in many situations. Prayer is especially important because you could never know what someone is going through in life. Sometimes you may not know what to do but Prayer can really help them. I love to pray because it helps me when I need it the most. Praying is like talking to God. Sometimes we may feel distant from Him at times but just pray. He is sheets listening when no one else seems to be listening. I love to talk to God to tell him things about my day. I let all my emotions out to him. He is there when I need him the most. Praying to him is like talking to a father about things you need to let go of. When you contact your earthly father, your Heavenly Father is always nearby.

Prayer helped me at my lowest when I was getting bullied. I was so sad every day, my behavior kept changing. I was tired of being bullied so I prayed, and God helped me to overcome my fears and speak up to an adult about what I was going through. God helped me not get bullied after that. I was so happy. Prayer also helps when

I feel Alone at times. It helps me be comforted. Prayer also helps me if I am sick, sad, or mad! If you ever need to talk someone or feel alone, or it seems like no one cares! Just pray to God! He will never let you down or He will never leave you nor forsake you ever.

# ABOUT THE INTERCESSOR

## Dr. Monique Rodgers

Dr. Monique Rodgers is an ordained prophet, visionary, intercessor, international best-selling author, CEO, motivational speaker, entrepreneur, educator, and literary genius. Dr. Rodgers excels today as a notable writing coach, founder, pioneer, and serial entrepreneur.

Throughout the course of her career, she has written such prolific works as, Hello! My name is Millennial, picking up the pieces, The Majestical land of Twinville, falling in love with Jesus, Accelerate, Overcoming Writer's Block, just breathe, and called to intercede volumes 1-8. She has also been included as a co-author in collaborations such as, Jumpstart Your Mind, Speak Up We deserve To Be Heard, Finding Joy in the Journey Volume 2, Let the Kingdompreneurs Speak, and My sister helped me heal. Due to her outstanding breadth of experience, dr. rodgers has been featured on radio shows, podcasts, and has hosted her own radio show and tv show. She has graced several platforms worldwide. She served as a tv host for WATCTV Atlanta. she has been featured in heart and soul magazine, my story the magazine, kish magazine's top twenty national authors of 2021. marquis who is who in America 2021-2022. She also assisted in various volunteer work including an executive team member for lady delivers arise with Apostle Bianca Lawry. She is an also on the board of directors for I am my sister organization. She is also a certified master business coach and vegan health coach. she has served on various leadership positions in business and in ministry. she is currently a prayer hub leader for the city of Raleigh under the tutelage of Apostle Jennifer LeClaire. she is also an ambassador for kingdom sniper institute with evangelist Latrice Ryan. she is also a social media manager for Patricia Bailey ministries. She is a team member of CBK with ambassador Sofia Ruffin. Dr. Rodgers earned her undergraduate degree at Oral Roberts

University. She obtained her master's degree and doctorate degree from Colorado Technical University. She is a global leader that has also studied at The Black Business School online as well as Harvard Business School online. Dr. Rodgers intends to expand upon her expertise and continue serving God in ministry. She aspires to help over one hundred authors to complete and publish their books and to help intercessors to draw closer to God.

Chapter 6

# Prayers For Women That Desire Children

## Dr. Monique Rodgers  Visionary

The most array of sound that you can ever hear and listen to is that of a child's laughter. There is such a purity in the giggles and the fun that are included with the beautiful sounds of laughter. There is such an innocence and pure love that permeates from it, have you ever found yourself to be in a place of such longing for a life much for fulfilling than the one that you are currently living?

That was my prayer several years ago and it remains one of my greatest prayers now for the amazingly simple fact that I was created to live and to also pass on my legacy to my future children and my children's children for the future generations. I have been the single barren woman that has prayed for children to leave a legacy to for generations to follow. In Psalm 127:3-5 it states that, "Sons are the heritage from the Lord, children are a reward from him. Like arrows in the hands of a warrior are sons born in one's youth. Blessed is the man whose quiver is full of them. They will not be put to shame when they contend with their enemies in the gate." In Proverbs 17:6

it acclaims children as, "Children's children are a crown to the aged, and parents are the pride of their children." Children bring so much life and joy to our lives.

When I was a teacher for elementary school and for middle school my greatest joy was being able to educate and to teach children. Each opportunity in the classroom to teach was also showing the love of God in my classroom. Each morning I would come in early and pray over each locker of my students, then I would pray and play worship music in my classroom before the students arrived and anoint all their seats with oil. Although I have never had any children of my own, I have found such delight in educating children in not only in America, but I have also taught English online for children in China. It created a diversity of understanding for me as it pertained to children. My heart would often grow saddened when I was ever around parents who did not appreciate or even love their children. Children are a gift from God that comes with great responsibility and love. Our priority is to show love to the children through nurturing them and ensuring that their basic needs are being met. There are many women in my friendship circle from college that are also waiting and praying to one day have children of their own.

The other day I received a box of Similac powdered milk in the mail with gift cards for baby items. I thought to myself did someone send this as a prank. I do not have any children. Then I paused for a second and begin to get teary eyed because I said God, I have prayed for years to have a child, but my request has seemed to have gone unheard. The milk box was a sign to me that God has not forgotten about me and that in the appointed time he will send my husband and I will be able to have children that I can cherish and love that are my own. My prayer for those that are reading this chapter and you may have become discouraged or weary in seeing your prayers become answered. Do not give up on your prayers no matter what it looks like now God will always provide an answer to us. It may be yes, no, or bur He will always answer us when we listen to him speak.

Father in the name of Jesus, I pray for all the single women, divorced, widowed, and all the women that have ever wanted children and have not been able to give birth to any yet. I pray God that if it be your will that you will send them a husband to bring forth children with to love and to celebrate together. I pray for open wombs of promise to be upon your daughters. I pray for healing for women that have been barren, have lost children, have not been able to conceive children that that you would give them miracle babies.

I decree and declare blessed children and families, I decree and declare children that are a loved, I decree and declare children are celebrated and cherished. I decree and declare children that are affirmed and prayed for. I decree and declare children that are educated and instructed well in knowledge and in the word of God.

I decree and declare that families will pray together again and love one another. I decree and declare that children are the promise from God. I decree and declare that parents will be obedient unto the Lord and hear the instruction and provide safe answers to children. I decree and declare children that are history makers and nation shakers for God that will not compromise but live lives that are honorable and in integrity. I decree and declare children that will not be succumbed to peer pressure or schemes, but they will be full of wisdom and grace.

I decree and declare children that are well cultured and have love for other nations. I decree and declare children that love their siblings and that love to share and give to others. I decree and declare children that are full of God's love, heart, and compassion. I decree and declare children that honor and love their parents and guardians. I decree and declare open wombs to all that have been closed to receive and to overflow in this season with greater faith for children.

# ABOUT THE INTERCESSOR

## Nicole Marrow

Nicole is A Spiritual Life Coach with Cole's Inc. In this role, Nicole looks after/coordinates/manages/leads a team providing Prayer in all aspects of Coaching, including Life, Business, and Accountability.

A big believer in F.A.I.T.H., Nicole supports other likeminded Spiritual Coaches.

Nicole Morrow is qualified as a Life Coach and holds the Certification from Accelerate Your Lives Coaching Program.

Nicole is no stranger to Coaching, having spent years as a Sales Representative and A Consultant where she motivated Boss Women to work ON their Businesses and IN their Businesses by uplifting them in Prayer and partnering with the Holy Spirit.

Nicole has more than eight years of coaching experience in Business.

Nicole helps Boss Women to grow and scale their businesses by keeping them accountable with motivation and Prayer. Nicole offers a wide range of programs and services, from Accountability, to F.A.I.T.H. restoration and Life Coaching. After a successful career in Spiritual Gifting, Nicole now coaches/teaches/advises Like-minded Boss Women and other people how to achieve the same success.

Passionate about Helping others, coaching and its possibilities, Nicole provides Spiritual services that help small businesses and those who choose to grow their businesses and be productive and accountable.

Nicole has been writing for many years and has maintained her own Company for eight years, successfully partnered with Direct Sales companies and collaborated, among others.

Chapter 7

# Short Prayers from the Heart

## Nicole Morrow

Father God prayer should not be a chore but a delight. Today I thank you for your goodness to me, for reaching out and finding me. Help me to see prayer as an intimate relationship with you. Amen

Father God,

You are so mighty, So, perfect. I praise your sovereignty. I have no idea what to do but my eyes are on you. I need you so much. I need your wisdom. I need your guidance. I am so incapable of leading my life. Please shine your light on my path. Amen

Father God,

I pray that you will help me, to go and focus on you... to worship you in Spirit and Truth. I Thank you, for all your goodness and kindness. Thank you, for this beautiful day. I will give it to you. Bless your name. Amen

Father God,

Please forgive me of all my sin. I feel so far away from you. I ask that you Renew and Revive me, may there be nothing between us.

Please deal with my heart. Help me to be more of a

Prayer Warrior. Amen Father God, I need you.

I pray that I will always look upward and outward. I pray that you would forgive my envious heart. Teach me to trust you more that I would never be discontent with what you send from your hand. Amen

Father God,

You are the Giver of good and perfect gifts. I love you. I Thank You for all the love you have for me, all the love you have shown me. I pray that you will lead and guide me. I ask that you have your way. Amen

Father God,

Please help me to follow your will. Help me to love you more and allow you to love me. I do not want to deceive myself. Please make me a usable vessel in your hands. I have so much to be Thankful for as I read your word. Thank you for your Grace and Mercy. Amen

Father God,

Open my eyes and heart to see and receive all that you have for me. Thank you for being so gracious and loving. Thank

You that you desire the truth of the heart. Amen

Father God,

I Thank you for who you are. I Thank you for loving me unconditionally, though I fail you. I want to know you and I really want to make you known. You are worthy of my praise and adoration. Amen

Father God,

My mind and heart are so unsettled. Help me to center myself on you. I love you, but I do not love you the way I should. Forgive me for loving the world more. I want to be the person you want me to be. Amen

Father God,

Help me to bring purity to my heart, mind, and Life. I want to love more with an awareness of your presence. Please allow me to be a Blessing of Encouragement to those in need of it. Help me to see the way you do. I want to love wholeheartedly. Amen

Father God,

I want my life to point others to you. I pray that you will have your way. That you would lead and direct my movement. Help me to quiet myself and sit before you today. I pray all distractions will be removed as I read your word and pray. Amen Father God,

Thank you for the Blessings ahead. As I spend time alone soaking in your presence. I pray that you would help me to hear, understand, receive, and apply all you say. Amen

Father God,

I lay everything in your hands. I am anxious but, I believe in your power and goodness, and I believe in your praise worthiness.

Thank you for loving me. You have put gladness in my heart.

Amen

Father God,

I feel like I have failed you sometimes. I feel lost. I pray that you will restore me. You know my needs before I ask. I am nothing without your will. Please forgive me and wash me in your blood.

Amen

Father God,

I am guilty, always guilty. Always facing condemnation apart from you. I have hope. There is no condemnation. You are my

righteousness. Please use me. Despite all my many weaknesses and failures. Shape me into the image of Jesus. Forgive me for not living wisely, I pray for revival. Amen

Father God,

You are my Great provider. I lift you up. Open my eyes to the great need of you. I ask that you go to work on my behalf. I ask that you open a door so that I can share you with others. May your will be done. I ask that you Encourage and Strengthen me. I ask that you keep me positive and Uplifted in your Spirit. Amen Father God,

Help me to stay a loving person, to help me be more caring. I want to be someone who displays your fruit. The fruit of your Holy Spirit. Amen

Father God,

Today, I pause to remember your goodness and take stock of the acts of grace you are performing in my life. Please cultivate in me a spirit of gratitude. You are my everything. Amen

Father God,

I know you. Open every door for me that I am not looking for and do not know that I need. According to the richness of your grace, Please Hear my Prayers. So, that my life may accord with your will.

Father God,

I ask that you keep my mind from knowing hatred or thinking the worst. I never want to feel jealous or judgmental. I pray that you work in the most powerful way and let me be a light to those around me. Amen

Father God,

I pray that you would settle my mind and my heart, that I may be prepared to receive from you. You are Loved,

Appreciated and Worthy to be praised. In Jesus Mighty and Holy name. AMEN

# ABOUT THE INTERCESSOR

**Prophetess Venesia Williams**

Prophetess Venesia Williams is a mother, Prophetess, The UK's number #1 Prophetic Empowerment Coach,

Global Keynote Speaker, Best Selling Author, Kingdom Entrepreneur, Investor and co-founder of The Power of Love Ministry, Empowering Women to Win Network, The Empowerment Club Ltd

Venesia is committed to proclaiming the Good News to the nations by any means necessary. Taking social media by storm continuously over the past several years Venesia spreads the gospel and empowers people daily through her pop-up prophetic empowerment broadcasts designed to encourage, edify, and win souls to the Kingdom of God.

Venesia is also on a mission to empower one million women to win in every single area of their lives, mentally, spiritually, physically and financially through her private one on one consultations, group empowerment coaching session, master classes and multiple streams of income business opportunities available www.venesiawilliams.com

# Chapter 8

# Breaking The Silence

## Prophetess Venesia Williams

Heavenly Father I come before you today to give you thanks and honor, I cover every parent reading this chapter today under the precious blood of Jesus as we join forces with the Power of the Holy Spirit to stand in the gap for all the children connected directly and in directly.

As we ask by faith Lord hear our requests as we seek you Lord meet us right where we are

Lord as we are knocking Lord open the doors to us according to your word in Matthew 7:7

As I was praying to the Lord, I heard him say I AM BREAKING THE SILENCE

Today is the day The LORD is Breaking the Silence as I stand in the gap for all the children suffering in silence

I put all our children before the King of Kings and the Lord of Lords today, the enemy tried to take our children's voices by consuming them with fear, doubt, anxiety, and low self-esteem.

But today I decree that our children are all being set free from all fear, doubt, and bondage, according to His word in 2 Timothy 1:17 God has not given us a spirit of fear, but gives us power, love, and sound mind.

I decree that every chain that has held our children captive is broken now in the mighty name of Jesus Christ.

I pray for divine protection and supernatural release for all the children suffering silently in child abuse, neglect, child sex trafficking, child exploitation, gang violence, battling self-sabotaging thoughts, self-harm, premature death.

Heavenly Father defends our children Lord God I pray that you hide all our children from the people who seek to exploit them, I pray that God will eliminate the plans and plots of the enemy concerning our children. Hear and answer our children cries for help remove the muzzles that has been silencing them and lose their tongues right now Lord thank you for breaking the silence today. I release the blood of Jesus to cover and protect our children from abductors that prey on the most vulnerable children according to your word Lord dispatch your angels to protect our children, recue those being led away to death; hold back those staggering towards slaughter (Proverbs. 24:11)

We call them back now from the four corners of the earth I decree our children are coming back from east, west, north, and south, we call them back into a safe place in you Lord. Jeremiah 31:16-17

(amp)

"Thus say the LORD: Refrain your voice from weeping, and your eyes from; for your (raising of your children, prayer) shall be rewarded, says the Lord, and they (your children) shall come back from the land of the enemy. There is hope (something you expect) in your future, says the LORD, that children shall come back to their own border (place of peace, safety, and well-being)."

I take authority over the enemy right now and decree that our children will be free from all guilt and shame, they will not be ashamed of where God has delivered them from, but they will walk power and in liberty and know the power of their testimony with the blood of the living lamb is a weapon against the enemy. The enemy wants to steal their identity that is why he keeps attacking them because he is trying to eventually let them be worn out but today, I release new strength Lord mount our children. up with wings like an eagle do not let them become weary or faint.

Heavenly father I pray you sanitize our children with the blood of Jesus, I pray for healing and restoration Father forgive the for any doors they have opened to the enemy knowingly or unknowingly through the desires of flesh, we put our children flesh on the altar today, Lord kill their flesh and let them be led by your spirit of truth not their flesh, I bind up the powers of darkness and take authority over every temptation, promiscuity and spirit of lust. Cleanse our children's minds against every imagination that exalts itself over you. Lord, we present our children's bodies to you as a living sacrifice, I speak total wholeness over their lives and cut off every ungodly soul-ties or covenant made against your will, Lord purifies their hearts and free them from any sexual brokenness caused by abuse or their own actions. I pray our children will have self-control and patience they will not be involved in any form of sexual intimacy outside marriage, nor will they indulge in pornography, sexual fantasies, oral sex, masturbation we renounce it now in Jesus Name.

Today, Lord, I invite you into our children's pain to heal them with your love. Today I claim our children's healing, peace, joy, and strength in any area that they are weak let them be made strong, Jesus fills our children with your holiness take off the heavy garments and place upon our children the garments of praise and the robe of righteousness.

Lord I pray that our children will find their identity in Christ and not gangs, disconnect and deliver them from all gang activity, Lord you see our communities being overrun by gang violence but today I pray for peace and I thank you Lord for your Son through Him our children can become a new creation, we claim the blessings of the peacemakers upon our children today according to Matthew 5:9 Help our children see themselves the way you see them, so they can help bring peace and hope to our communities let our children be the example of Christ and the light in the midst of all the darkness in the world, the earth is crying out for the manifestations of the sons of God. Lord, I thank you for the wisdom to train up our children in the way they should go and when they get old, they will not depart from that way.

I decree power to all the vulnerable children right now Lord recue and deliver them from the wicked according to your word in Psalm 82:3-4

Defend the poor and fatherless; Do justice to the afflicted and needy.

Deliver the poor and needy Free them from the hand of the wicked.

I decree Isaiah 54:13

"All your sons will be taught by the LORD, and great will be your children's peace."

I decree Isaiah 49:6-7 (amp)For I will contend with him who contends with you, And I will save (defend, preserve, rescue, deliver) Your children.

Lord, we know that you love us and love our children you said in your word in Matthew 19:14

"LET THE LITTLE CHILDREN COME TO ME AND DO NOT HINDER THEM, FOR THE KINGDOM OF

HEAVENBELONGS TO THEM.

As I was interceding for our children I felt an earthquake in the spirit just like when Paul and Silas was in prison and as they focused on

God and began to worship the Lord there was a sudden earthquake and then suddenly all their chains was loosed suddenly even those surrounding them were also set, I decree as you are reading this that all the children connected to you who are suffering in silence will be set free, the padlock that the enemy was using to lock their mouths has been broken and every tongue has been loosed today in Jesus Mighty Name.

I pray for boldness, strength and faith today as our children step out cover them under your precious blood Lord let no weapon formed against them prosper, let every negative word spoken over our children be condemned now, set our children free from every false label placed upon them, we come out of agreement with the lies of enemy and cancel the contracts made in hell we release the fire of God to consume them now and we come in total agreement and alignment with God's original plans for our children that are good and full of hope and a future.

Lord, I decree our children will know your goodness and provision, I pray they will always find their identity in you Lord and know that you are faithful through both challenges and joys in life. I ask even in the pressures of life Lord, it will not break them, but it will break them through to a new level of victory and they will know that you are their rock on which they stand. I pray through trials in life that you will guide them and bring them comfort. I decree our children will follow after you and be a builder of your kingdom, I pray our children will follow your voice and be children of great character seeking after your heart, build up the confidence within them to seek you boldly stir up a fresh fire a fresh hunger and a thirst for righteousness will spring forth from our children, a righteousness that leads our children to the renewing of minds, I pray for the power of God's love with consume our children today and they will experience the transformational power of God. I thank you Lord that the former things are being passed away and you are springing forth something new within our children and your original plan will be done and you will touch them again Lord and grow the fruits of the Spirit within them. Thank you, Jesus, that you have lived here as one of us, you know what it is like to be a child and can relate to everything that our children are feeling, you understand the language of their tears and I thank you today you are not only healing them, but you are making them whole. Thank you, Lord, that we are not alone but you are strategically parenting with us and equipping us with everything that we need to encourage, love, provide and nurture our children even in the times of uncertainty in life Lord you have already have good plans for our children filled with hope and a future as stated in Jeremiah 29:11.

Heavenly father I thank you that I can trust you for the future of our families, thank you Lord for continuing to guide our children please keep them safe and order their footsteps. Our children are a precious gift from God, praying for your children as a parent is one of the most powerful things you can do. Be encouraged today that God is in full control of everything including our children. Just remember that all things God works for the good of those who love him, who have been called and encourage them through your word, I surrender them to you Lord let them feel your presence and know that they are not alone, but you are with them and will never leave r forsake them. Lord let your deliverance be their bread today, uproot every demonic spiritual seed planted by the enemy and fill them up with an overflow of your Holy Spirit leaving no room from the enemy to return. I thank you in advance for saving them and for setting them free for them experiencing your transformational power of GOD to divinely restore them and reconcile them back to Him.

# ACKNOWLEDGMENTS

I want to firstly acknowledge God who is the head of my life and thank Him for using me as His vessel and covering me daily under His wings of protection and calling me to be a woman of prayer and for blessing me with my children that are truly the fuel to my fire to make my house a house of prayer. I would also like to acknowledge my mother Pastor Mauverlyn Whittaker who has been a true example of a praying mother, if it had not been for her prayers, I would not be the woman in God I am today. I would also like to thank Dr Monique for giving me this opportunity to be a part of this powerful book collaboration my desire is to see our children set free and living life on purpose and I believe through prayer we will see the change we want to see.

# ABOUT THE INTERCESSOR

Peshon Allen is a servant and believer in Jesus Christ, a Wife, Mother, Worship Leader, Psalmist and Speaker. She is a Bestselling Author, an Army Veteran, an alumnus of American Forces Broadcast Network and a licensed minister. Peshon is the Founder of "Women in Ministry on The Move" podcast. An immensely popular online radio show that celebrates and empowers women from all levels of society and services they provide in ministry and their communities. Her heart and mandate have always been winning souls for Christ and to preach the gospel to the lost, to save the lost at all costs. Her belief is Prayer is essential and key for every believer. It is our open line of communication with God our Father and it very vital, necessary, and precious. A Christian without a prayer life is like a human body without air.

# Chapter 9

# Praying for Children

## Mrs. Peshon Allen

When we see our children or any children running around and we investigate their faces, see their smiles, and hear their laughter, we are looking at the face, reward, and love of God the Father. God loves children. In fact, He loves children so much that he calls them our reward and our blessings from Him. The Bible says in Psalm 127:3 (The Message), "Don't you see children are God's best gift?

The fruit of the womb his generous legacy? Like a warrior's fistful of arrows are the children of a vigorous youth. Oh, how blessed are you parents, with your quivers full of children! Your enemies do not stand a chance against you; you will sweep them right off your doorstep." It is God who opens the womb and blesses the barren woman to become fruitful. There are many instances in the Bible where God promised children to families and barren women cried out to God for children and He answered their prayers by blessing them with the children they asked for, the fruit of the womb. God told Abraham and Sarah, He was going to give them a son and then told them what to name the child. Children are Intentionally from

God and have purpose and great destiny. Hannah cried out to God for a child and God gave her Samuel the prophet according to 1 Samuel 1:10-19 (King James Version). I said all of that to say this, if God the Father is the one who gives us children and calls them gifts and rewards; and tells us according to Proverbs 22:6, (The King

James Version), "Train up a child in the way he should go: and when he is old, he will not depart from it." Then He commands us and our children, he does not ask us anything, but commands not only us, but our children according to Ephesians 6:1-4, "Children, obey your parents in the Lord: for this is right. Honor thy father and mother; which is the first commandment with promise; That it may be well with thee, and thou mayest live long on the earth. And ye fathers, provoke not your children to wrath: but bring them up in the nurture and admonition of the Lord." Then surely The Lord wants us to Pray for the children He has given to us. God is entrusting us with these beautiful innocent souls, to love them and to teach them about Him and all His wonderful works and loving kindness towards us all. The

Lord says in Deuteronomy 4:9, "Only be careful and watch yourselves closely so that you do not forget the things your eyes have seen or let them fade from your heart if you live. Teach them to your children and to their children after them.

Father God, there is no one greater than You! There is no one who loves us, saves us, heals us like You do. We come is agreement with

Your Word and thank You for every child born and that you have given into our care in the Name of Jesus. Father, we pray a hedge of protection around our children and that You would protect them from the evil one. I thank You that according to Isaiah 54:13-16, (The King James version) "And all thy children shall be taught of the Lord; and great shall be the peace of thy children. In righteousness shalt thou be established: thou shalt be far from oppression; for thou shalt not fear and from terror; for it shall not come near thee. Behold, they shall surely gather, but not by me: whosoever shall gather against thee shall fall for thy sake. Behold, I have created the smith that bloweth the coals in the fire, and that bringeth forth an instrument for his work; and I have created the waster to destroy. No weapon that is formed against thee shall prosper; and every tongue that shall rise against thee in judgment thou shalt condemn. This is the heritage of the servants of the Lord, and their righteousness is of me, saith the Lord." I decree and declare Psalm 34:7 over their lives, that the angel of the Lord encamps around our children because they fear You and reverence you and you deliver them from all things. Our children shall complete every purpose you created them for in

Jesus Name. For as Jeremiah 1:5 says, "Before I formed thee in the belly, I knew thee; and before thou camest forth out of the womb I sanctified thee, and I ordained thee a prophet unto the nations." Lord helps us to be living examples for our children to imitate and live holy as You are holy. Lord God, no matter what we or our children may go through in this life, I pray that they are strong and unmovable in their faith. I thank You that our children know You and Your word and will hid it in their hearts that they might not ever sin against

You. I decree that our children are led by Your Spirit and will follow

Your leading and guiding them all the days of their lives. Thank You Father God that our children are wise beyond their years and will not be led astray by their peers and they will not give in to peer pressure.

Lord, I pray for godly friendships for our children and not anyone that will have a negative influence over them in the name of

Jesus.

Thank you for placing godly, wise friends in their lives, all the days of their lives. Father God, we decree and declare that our children are blessed. They are healed. They are delivered, saved, and set free.

They are more than conquerors through Christ Jesus that loves them!

I thank You Father God and declare over our children, according to

Romans 8:38-39, (King James version), For I am persuaded, that neither death, nor life, nor angels, nor principalities, nor powers, nor things present, nor things to come, Nor height, nor depth, nor any other creature, shall be able to separate them from the love of God, which is in Christ Jesus our Lord. And 1 John 5:14, we have this confidence that, if we ask any thing according to Your will, Lord, you hear us: And if we know that You hear us, whatsoever we ask, we know that we have the petitions that we desired of You. Thank

You Father God for Your loving kindness towards us and I decree and declare that our children do not walk in the counsel of the ungodly, but their delight is in the law of the Lord, and they meditate day and night in it. They are like a tree planted by the rivers of water, which brings forth their fruit in their season, and their leaves do not wither and whatsoever they do Lord shall prosper. We pray this prayer over our children for generations to come until the end of time in Jesus Name Amen and Amen.

# ABOUT THE INTERCESSOR

## PASTOR CLARA COHEE-RUSSELL

Pastor Clara Cohee-Russell: Founder & CEO of REACH Women 4 God Ministries, which is now Women Walking in Wisdom. She is a woman after God's own heart, called and chosen of God to preach the word of God in the highways and byways; reaching out to a dying world sharing what thus says the Lord. She is a prayer warrior, an exhorter, mentor, certified transformational life coach, worshipper, Entrepreneur, and five-time published author.

Pastor Cohee-Russell worked as an Evangelist serving in ministry since she was a young child growing up in the C.O.G.I.C. background, singing in the choir, teaching Sunday School, and singing on the Praise Team. Pastor Russell was saved at the early age of 5 years old, she was saved and filled with the Holy Ghost with the evidence of speaking in tongues at the age of thirteen. Pastor Russell was totally sold out to Christ at the age of 28 years old and began working in full capacity.

Pastor Cohee started working as a servant in her church where she served for 19 years in different auxiliaries, a faithful choir member and praise team member and worked in clerical positions and she answered her call as an Evangelist and is now serving as Assistant Pastor in ministry with her husband who is the Pastor of Iron Sharpening Iron Ministries.

Co-Founder/Administrative Officer of Iron Sharpening Iron Ministries 501c (3)

Founder/CEO Butterfly Life Mentoring & MNM Coaching

Founder of The Praying Mothers of Inmates Prayer Ministry

Founder/CEO of Women Walking in Wisdom

President of Precious Sister Women's Ministry

President of WCC Women's Ministry

Volunteer Coordinator over Helps Ministry

Church web site coordinator

Praise Dancer & Drama Team

Praise Team Leader

Choir Member and Secretary

Intercessory Prayer Team

Sunday School Teacher

VBS Teacher

Hospitality & Usher Board

President of Sunshine Band

Chairperson of MLH Scholarship Committee

WCC

Pastor Russell later was married Oct. 16, 2010, upon which her and her husband Pastor Harold Russell began to operate in their callings from God together. Shortly after their marriage God birthed a Women's Ministry in Pastor Cohee-Russell which is still being molded into a final work for the Lord; Pastor Cohee-Russell has served as a Sunday School Teacher, she served as President of WCC-Women's Christian Council, where she hosted her first women's conference which was an enormous success in the Lord in 2012.

She has served on the Praise Team and as a Choir member and served on the Missionary Board.

Pastor Cohee- Russell was licensed as an Evangelist and worked as unto the Lord doing street ministry, feeding those who are less fortunate and the homeless, handing out personal hygiene bags, going into the prisons teaching, and preaching the word of God.

God elevated Pastor Cohee-Russell and her husband Pastor Harold Russell to Pastors of ISIM (Iron Sharpening Iron Ministries) with boots on the ground. Carrying the word, giving clothing, hygiene bags and food to those on the street corners in the parking lots, sharing the word to those in the prisons, in the juvenile detention centers and wherever God leads, being true foot soldiers for Christ.

# Chapter 10

# When a Mother Prays

## Pastor Clara Cohee-Russell

I grew up in a small town in Texas, where people sat out on the porch and waved at friends and neighbors as they passed by. Well, I have always been what people would call a church girl. My mother kept my sisters and my brother and I in church most of the time. So, singing and giving God praise was a natural thing for me. However, prayer was for the preacher, ministers, or missionaries to do. I did many jobs in the church as I got older, like being an usher, Sunday school teacher for the toddlers, helping with the Sunshine Band for the smaller children and helping to prepare dinners for eating on the grounds. But again, praying was not one of the things I did in the church. I did however have a prayer life at home. It was concise prayers; little did I know they would soon be more than that.

As I grew up into my young adult life, I began to encounter real life problems and situations. Life as I knew it as a young child was no more. My mother died when I was sixteen years old, and my siblings all were married and moved away. My Dad remarried and left me alone in the house I grew up in. He was still there in town, whenever I needed him all I had to do was call him, but at the same time I was alone.

As I grew older and made grown up decisions for myself it was then that I decided to move to a larger city not too far from home but far enough that I would have to learn to navigate on my own in life. Although I say my own, God was always with me, I just did not realize it yet.

I found myself working, paying my own bills, and making my way, but I was in a relationship that really would never go anywhere even though I thought he was going to be my husband and we would have children and live a wonderful life. Well, how many of you know that is not how things worked out?

I got a good paying job and had my own apartment, but he just kept running in and out of my life. He was there when it was convenient for him, and he had nowhere else to go. But whenever he found another woman to lie down with that seemed like she had a little more money or more substance that would help him to come up in this world he was off and gone again.

I tell everyone that shacking up (which was a term used when I was younger, and you were living with your boyfriend or girlfriend, but you were not married) got me nothing but pregnant and left behind. However, because of the relationship and how it was going I prayed to God to give me somebody that would love me and never leave me and would always love me back unconditionally the way I loved them.

Well God heard my prayer and He allowed me to get pregnant. That was the beginning of a prayer life with God. I still at that point did not realize the power of prayer and the connection it gives you with the father. I remember my Pastor's wife from my old church telling me we pray for our children all their lives. They move from your lap to your heart. I did not understand all of that either not fully until it became a matter of the heart for me.

As I got older and began to realize the power of prayer and that I had a prayer life with God and He hears me when I pray, I began to take prayer much more seriously. I began to study the word of God finding out more about who I was and what my purpose was, and I would pray, and God would answer when I prayed at home. But I joined a church that had designated days for the ministers to pray, the elders to pray and the evangelists to pray. Well, I was in that rotation. I would pray but because of words I had heard spoken about me as I grew in church, I felt inadequate to pray in a church setting.

But nonetheless I was in rotation, and I had to pray. Well, the church formed an intercessory prayer wall and only a few people were praying so I volunteered that if needed I would stand in to pray whenever they did not have anyone. I did not know it was a setup from God. They did not have anyone and so I was there to help with that prayer wall. I would pray and the palms of my hands would sweat terribly bad.

One day I was at a revival with my Pastor's wife and members of our church in a whole other state, and my Pastor's wife asked me to come up and pray. Well not only was I not at home praying over the phone and not at our home church even, but I was also at a different church in another state and extremely nervous. But as I began to pray, I could hear my Pastor's wife praying in my ear covering me in prayer as I prayed, and the fear broke off me and I began to go forth praying and interceding for others.

Like I said I always prayed on my own one on one with God at home and I know He heard me when I prayed because things would change. But when that fear broke off, I began to pray like I never have before. I began to pray from my heart for my children because when a mother prays things change.

I remember hearing my mother pray all the time as I was growing up. She would pray and worship and set the atmosphere in our home. Now the mantel has been passed on to me and I pray, praise & worship always.

I remember the words spoken off your lap and on your heart. God hears the wailing mothers that cry out for their children and their children's children. When a mother prays late in the midnight hour calling on the names of their children God spares lives. He blocks accidents and mechanical failures.

When a mother praise God heals bodies from chronic illnesses, sickness, and disease. When a mother praise God gives an ear to hear so that souls are saved, healed, and delivered.

When a mother prays grace and mercy fall upon our children and our children's children and they are blessed.

God hears the heart of a mother and for that I am grateful. I know God hears me when I pray.

The word tells us to honor our mothers and our fathers. Know that your mother is standing in the gap for you and has been from the time you were in the womb.

Show love to all the mothers that pray. Prayer will keep us, prayer will sustain our minds when the enemy would to come in like a flood to take us out, know that a mother is praying.

# Ways to Stay Connected

Follow Called to Intercede International on Instagram @CalledtoIntercede

Connect with Called to Intercede International on Facebook

Email us your prayer requests and praise reports to calledtointercede@gmail.com

Connect with us online https://www.calledtointerecede.com

Text the word PRAYER to 919-568-5860

Made in the USA
Columbia, SC
19 May 2022